The Tao Te Ching

Lao Tze

DEDICATION

To Robert, a master of light and darkness.

CONTENTS

Introduction

The Tao Te Ching is a work of many meanings, yet it is marked by a transparent clarity.

The paradoxical stances, assertions of the Tao Te Ching can be difficult, strange, head shaking in our place and time. Some may be bothered, even fearful. Others see in it the spectacular or fantastic.

It advocates seeming contradictions like wisdom with emptiness. Assertion is seen as weak, submission as empowering. Beauty is vested in the ugly. Words are used but seen as basically misleading. It states that winning and overcoming are at odds with competing and taking sides.

What are we to make of these seeming paradoxes? Is it merely a game, a word-game, a tautological nothing? Where, if any, topicality or "substance" is in the work?

There have been hundreds of translations and adaptations of the Tao Te Ching. Each unique and seemingly contradictory as the Tao Te Ching itself. This version attempts to give a simple and plain version of the Tao Te Ching updated for current times. For the Tao Te Ching is still very relevant and even topical. It speaks of great militaries, the role of women, economics, consumption, the environment, war, and politics. Humanity's relation to itself, science, and Heaven itself.

In an age where people have fallen into the rabbit-hole, like Alice into Wonderland, and nothing is what it appears to be, where right bleeds into wrong, beauty into the ugly, crime is cause, war is peace, is there anything the Tao Te Ching can do to teach us, aid us, succor us? What can the Tao Te Ching do to help us out of the rabbit-hole we've all fallen into?

Peter Kang

Tao Te Ching

PART 1

The Tao

The Way - Chapters 1 to 37

Chapter 1

The eternal Tao cannot be described in
symbols.
The name that can be symbolized is not
the eternal Name.

Heaven and Earth meet in a nameless
interface.
Symbolizing is the beginning of creation.

Freed from desire, you can see the
hidden marvels.
Desire masks the hidden.
Under the masking of desire you can
only see what is apparently real.

Yet marvels and reality
emerge from the same source.
This source is called darkness.

Darkness born from darkness.
The beginning of all understanding.

Chapter 2

Humans judge things as beautiful,
so ugliness is simultaneously created.
As humans judge things as good,
evil is simultaneously created.

Being and non-being are sides of a coin.
Difficult and easy are complementary.
Long and short are defined by each
other.
High and low are in opposition.
Fore and aft follow each other.

Therefore the Master can be effective
without action
and teach without words.
Things come his way and he does not
stop them;
things leave and he lets them go.
He has without possessing,
and acts without any expectations.
When his work is done, he takes no
credit.
That is why his influence will last
forever.

Chapter 3

If you over-esteem talented individuals,
people will value prizes and become too
competitive.
When property becomes too desired,
people will begin to steal.

Do not make a display of your riches
or envy will grow around you.

The Master leads by simplifying the
minds of people;
keeping food for their bellies,
reducing their ambitions,
and making them strong.
Prefer simplicity.
Prefer freedom from desire.
Avoid the pitfalls of knowledge and
wrong action.

For those who master the practice of
non-doing,
all fall into their proper place.

Chapter 4

The Tao is like an empty vessel:
it can never be completely empty or
completely filled.
Infinitely vast, it is the source of all
things.
It dulls what is too sharp, unties the
knotted,
gives shade to the hotly lit, and unifies
all creation with dust.

It is unseen but always present.
I do not know who the maker was.
It may be older than God.

Chapter 5

Heaven and Earth are not biased;
they treat all of creation as dogs in the
wind.
The Master doesn't take sides;
he treats everyone like dogs in the
wind.

The space between Heaven and Earth is
like a bellows;
it is empty, yet retains its power.
The more it is used, the more it
produces;
the more you talk of it, the further you
get to true comprehension.

It is better to be silent than to speak of
things you
do not understand.

Chapter 6

Emptiness as spirit is immortal.
It is like the great female,
because gives birth to both Heaven and
Earth.

Much like vaporous movement,
nearly invisible but always present.
Use it without effort.

Chapter 7

The Tao of Heaven is infinite,
and the earth is very long in time.
Why are they long lasting?
They are not selfish and live for
themselves;
thus they are present for all creatures.

The Master selflessly puts herself in the
rear;
And finds herself in the place of power.
She distances herself from all things;
Therefore she is unified with all things.
She gives no thought to self.
She is perfectly content.

Chapter 8

The greatest good is like water,
which benefits all of creation
without competing against it.
Like water, it gathers in unpopular,
unglamorous places.
Thus it is much like the Tao.

The location determines the value of the
residence.
Breadth of understanding makes a good
mind.
Good intention makes the gift good.
Integrity makes the government good.
Achieving makes your labors good.
Timeliness makes a decision good.

Only when there is no useless
competition
will we all live in peace.

Chapter 9

An empty cup is easier to handle
than a cup that is full.

The sharpest knives become the
quickest to fray.
The greater the wealth, the greater the
effort
to retain.
Pride is the source of its own turmoil.

Walk away from goals achieved, for the
basking
has its own pitfalls.
This way is the road to Heaven and
Progress.

Chapter 10

Understand and feed the darkness of
your soul
until you become whole.
To do this without failure is success.
Focus and learn of your breathing as to
become a newborn child.
Gaze deep into your soul and rewire
what is disconnected.
Love and lead people without forcing and
pressuring them.
When Heaven gives and takes without
reason, accept the outcome without
rancor.
When you think you've understood all
things, step back from that
understanding.

Giving birth and nourishing,
making without possessing,
expecting nothing in return.
To grow, yet not to control:
This is the mysterious virtue.

Chapter 11

Thirty spokes are connected to the
wheel,
but it is the empty center axis that
allows
the wheel to function.

We mold clay into a pot,
but it is the empty space inside
that makes the vessel useful.

We fashion wood for a house,
but it is the empty space inside
that provides the living area.

Therefore, the substantial space is what
is created.
But, it is the emptiness that we use.

Chapter 12

Five colors dull themselves in the eye.
Five notes deaden themselves in the ear.
Five flavors stale the taste on the tongue.
Too much stimulation bewilders the mind.
Too much money creates crime.

The Master acts with his inner eye, not on what he sees.
He lays aside the latter, and prefers to heed the former.

Chapter 13

Success creates dangers from and of
itself.
Our own enemies are often in the mirror.

What dangers to itself does success
create?
He who has power must also lose that
power.
Receiving favor and privilege causes
alarm and worry at their loss.
This is why success creates its own
dangers.
Why are we often our own worst
enemy?
It is the self that is an enemy of you, the
great you.
If I no longer had a "self", I would no
longer have an enemy.

Identify and love the world like it is you,
then you will truly care for all things.

Chapter 14

Try to focus upon it, and it can't be
clearly seen.
Try to listen for it, and it can't be heard.
Attempt to clutch it, it can't be gotten.
Further description is not possible in
these three ways,
so we will treat them as The One.

At its highest, it is not bright.
At its lowest depths, it is not dark.
Without end, without name, it returns to
nothingness.
Forms that are without forms.
Names that are without names.
Subtle, beyond understanding's reach.

Get closer and you will not find a
beginning,
trace it and you will not find the end.
By beginning to understand The Tao of
the ancients,

we can begin to comprehend our current selves.
To know the Tao as the ancients knew it is the beginning of wisdom.

Chapter 15

The ancient Sages were vastly profound.
Subtlety and discernment were part of
their nature.
They were wise beyond our own wisdom.
I can only give a poor representation of
their superior knowledge.

They were scrupulous as someone in
winter crossing an icy stream.
Alert and sensitive as if surrounded by
enemies in the forest.
Courteous as a guest with a respected
host.
Fluid as melting ice.
Whole as an uncut block of wood.
Receptive as a vast low lying valley.
Turbid like muddy waters.

Do you possess the patience for stillness
until the mud settles and water clears?
Can you remain patient until the right
moment avails itself?

The Master doesn't seek fulfillment.

For being un-full is a state useful in itself and gives a completion in itself.

Chapter 16

If you can empty your mind of all
thoughts, your heart will embrace
tranquility and peace.
Behold the mechanics of all creation,
watch as they return to their origins.

All creatures in the universe return to
where
they originated.
The return to our origins is tranquility
because Heaven mandated this to be.

Constancy is following Heaven's
mandates.
To know this constancy is called
enlightenment.
To not know this constancy is a source
of evil deeds

for it makes rootless.
By knowing the constant we can accept things as they are.
By accepting things as they are, we become impartial.
By being impartial, we become one with Heaven.
By being one with Heaven, we become one with Tao.
Being one with Tao, we are no longer concerned about losing our life because we know the Tao is constant and we are one with Tao.

Chapter 17

The best leaders lead without credit or
display so the people hardly know of
them.
The next best is a leader beloved by
people.
Leaders who use fear are worse.
And the hated leaders are the worst of
all.

The exercise of distrust makes
people untrustworthy.

The best leaders are careful and
conscious of frugally using words.
At the conclusion of his efforts, the
people say,
"The success was due to our efforts."

Chapter 18

When the great Tao is lost, charity,
sentiment, and righteousness appear.
When cleverness reigns, then hypocrisy
prevails.

When the family becomes weak, then
men invoke "brotherly love."

When the country falls into disorder and
dysfunction,
politicians shout "I am a patriot."

Chapter 19

Knowledge and wisdom are a burden to the people.
Throw away charitable giving and righteousness,
and people will return to brotherly love.
Throw away profit and greed,
and there won't be any thieves.

These three are superficial and aren't enough
to keep us at the center of the circle, so we must also:

Embrace simplicity.
Put others first.
Desire little.

Chapter 20

Renounce knowledge as it is a source of
endless problems.
What is the distance between a yes and
a no?
What is the distance between a good act
and a bad act?
Must you share the fears of others?
Ridiculous, you've missed the point by a
great deal.

Others are joyous and happy like at a
spring festival.
Only I am unconcerned and blank, like a
child who
hasn't been taught to smile.

Others possess expensive items and
property,

I possess nothing.
I drift about lost with no place to get to.
Like a dummy, I have no clear thoughts.

Everywhere people are bright;
I alone am dark.
Everywhere people are clever;
I alone am dull.
Everywhere people seem
discriminating;
I alone am muddled and confused.
I drift on the waves on the ocean,
blown at the mercy of the wind.
Everywhere people have their goals,
I alone am dull and uncouth.

I am different from people everywhere.
I nurse from the Great Mother's
breasts.

Chapter 21

The greatest virtue you can have
comes from following only the Tao;
which takes a form that is intangible and
evasive.

Even though the Tao is intangible and
evasive,
we are able to know it exists.
Intangible and evasive, yet it has a
manifestation.
Secluded and dark, yet there is vitality
within it.
Its vitality is very genuine.
Within it we can find order.

Since the beginning of time, the Tao has
always existed.
It is beyond existing and not existing.
How do I know where creation comes
from?
I look inside myself and see it.

Chapter 22

First, break yourself to become whole.
First, twist yourself to become straight.
First, empty yourself to become full.
First, become old to become new.
If your desires are weak, you will find
yourself.
If your desires are strong, you will lose
yourself.

For this reason the Master embraces the
Tao,
as an example for the world to follow.
As the Master is not self-centered,
people see him clearly.
As the Master is not boastful, people see
him as a shining model.
As he does not glorify himself, people
esteem him.
As he wants nothing from this world, the
world cannot defeat him.

When the ancient Masters said,
"Wanting to become whole,
then first let yourself be broken,"
they weren't using empty words.
All who do this will be made complete.

Chapter 23

Nature uses words sparingly:
a hard wind doesn't last long;
a heavy rain last but a little while.
What is the cause for this?
Heaven and Earth.

Why do humans go about without end,
when nature is succinct and short?
By opening yourself to the Tao,
you become one with it.
By opening yourself to Virtue,
you become virtuous.
By opening yourself to loss,
you will become lost.

Open yourself to the Tao,
the Tao will eagerly welcome you.
Open yourself to virtue,
virtue will become a part of you.
Open yourself to loss,
the lost are glad to see you.

"When you do not trust people,
people will become untrustworthy."

Chapter 24

People on their tiptoes stand wobbly.
People in a rush don't get far.
People who try to outshine others dim
themselves.
People who call themselves righteous
don't know how wrong they are.
People who brag about their
accomplishments reduce
themselves.

With the Tao as measure, these actions
are unworthy. To follow the Tao, we
must not do these things.

Chapter 25

Before the universe was born
there was something in the chaos of the
heavens.
It stands alone and empty,
solitary and unchanging.
It is ever present and secure.
It may be regarded as the Mother of the
universe.
Because I do not know its name,
I call it the Tao.
If forced to give it a name,
I would call it 'Great'.

Because it is Great means it is
everywhere.
Being everywhere means it is timeless.
Being timeless means everything returns
to it.

Tao is great.
Heaven is great.
Earth is great.
Humanity is great.
Within the universe, these are the four
great things.
Humanity follows Earth.
Earth follows Heaven.
Heaven follows the Tao.
The Tao follows only itself.

Chapter 26

The heavy is the basis of the light.
Stillness is the source of movement.

Thus the Master travels all day
without ever leaving his stock.
Even though he has much to see,
is he at peace and serene.

Why should the lord of a thousand
chariots
be amused at the foolishness of the
world?
If you abandon yourself to foolishness,
you lose touch with your origins.
If you let yourself become distracted,
you will lose the connection to yourself.

Chapter 27

Travel well and leave no tracks.
A skillful speaker avoids injury,
a good bookkeeper has an excellent
memory,
and a well-made door is easy to open
and is secure when closed.
A good knot needs no rope and won't
untie.
Thus the Master is willing to help
everyone,
and doesn't abandon others.
He is there to help all of creation,
from the great to the small.
This is called staying with the light.

So the good is a teacher to the bad.
The bad is the raw material for the
good.
By not honoring your teacher or by not
treasuring
your students you will become deluded
regardless
of your smarts.
This is the great secret.

Chapter 28

Know the male,
but keep to the female:
and become a watershed to the world.
If you are a watershed to the world
eternal youth will stay with you.

Know the white,
yet keep to the black:
be an example for the world.
If you are an example for the world,
the Tao will gain inside you and you will
return to your boundless beginnings.

Know the glory,
but keep to the humble:
receive the world as it is.
If you receive the world with
compassion
then your virtue will return you to the
Uncarved Block.

The block of wood is carved into
utensils
by carving void into the wood.
The Master uses the utensils, yet prefers
to keep to the block because of its
endless potential.
The great retains its boundless
possibilities.

Chapter 29

Is your ambition to control and rule the
world?
I see that such ambitions are fruitless.

The world is a sacred vessel
and it cannot be controlled.
The world defies control.
It slips and avoids your grasp in endless
ways.

Some are natural leaders,
and others are natural followers.
Some do things easily,
and others strain.
Some are big and strong,
and others are small and weak.
Some are protected and raised,
and others are destroyed.

The Master accepts the world as it is.
He eliminates the extremes.
Eliminates excess.
Eliminates arrogance.

Chapter 30

Those who lead people by following the
Tao
don't use soldiers to enforce their will.
Soldiers create opposing soldiers.

Where armies march, barbed wire and
munitions depots arise.
After armies take to war,
hard and difficult years must follow.
The wise commander makes a quick,
decisive
attack and ends the mission.
Take no pride in victories won through
war.
When war is won, arrogance must now
be fought.
War is the last alternative, victors should
take
no glee upon victory.
In time the strong always become
weak.

Military conquest is not the way of the
Tao.

What does not follow the Tao cannot survive.

Chapter 31

Weapons signal bad tidings;
all people should detest them.

The wise man values the left side,
and in time of war he values the right.
Weapons are made for destruction,
and wise men take care to avoid them.
When all else fails does the wise man
take up arms.
As peace is an objective,
war must be accepted with sadness.
Those who rejoice in war's victory
are delighting in the slaughter of
humanity.
Those who resort to violence
can never gain sustained peace.

The death of many should be greeted
with great sorrow,
and the victory celebration should honor
those who have died.

Chapter 32

The nameless, eternal Tao appears
insignificant,
but no power in the world can rule over
it.

A ruler following the Tao will soon
naturally lead his people.
Heaven would reign in his realm and
sweet rain descend from above.
People would need few laws for the laws
would be
written in their hearts.

While names are necessary for order,
naming itself can not create a justly
order.
Know the impersonal nature of naming.
Knowing when to stop naming is to be
free of its trappings.

The Tao is the end of all things.
Like the oceans it collects the flow of
rivers and streams.

Chapter 33

Those who know others are intelligent;
those who know themselves are truly
wise.
Those who master others are strong;
those who master themselves have true
power.

Those who know they have enough are
truly wealthy.
Those who persist will reach their goal.

Those who keep their course have a
strong will.
Those who die but do not perish are long
lasting.

Chapter 34

The great Tao flows unobstructed in
every direction.
All things rely on it to conceive and be
born,
and it does not deny even the smallest
of creation.
When it has accomplished great
wonders,
it does not claim them for itself.
It nourishes infinite worlds,
yet it doesn't seek to master the
smallest creature.
Since it is without wants and desires,
it can be considered humble.
All of creation seeks it for refuge
yet it does not seek to master or
control.
Because it does not seek greatness;
it is able to accomplish truly great
things.

Chapter 35

Follow the Tao and others will follow
your path.
You will go without fear of injury for the
peace and serenity of your mind cannot
be broken.

When there is bracing music and various
foods there is rejoicing and celebration
of partiers.

To them the words regarding the Tao
are tasteless and boring.

They see nothing when they look at the
Tao.
They hear nothing when they listen for
the Tao.
Yet, the Tao is always present and useful
for all.

Chapter 36

Do you want something to return to its
source?
Then spread it over a wide area.
Do you want a thing to weaken?
Then strengthen it vastly.
Do you wish to remove a thing?
Then allow it to flourish completely.
Wanting to possess something,
you must first give it away.

This is called the subtle understanding
of how things are aligned to the Tao.
The way the yielding can triumph over
the strong.

Just as fish hide in deep waters, the
state should not reveal its instruments of
power.

Chapter 37

The Tao never acts with force,
yet it is able to accomplish all.

If rulers could follow the way of the
Tao,
then all of creation would be
transformed.

If selfish desires arose with the
transformation I would
diminish them with the power of the
nameless Uncarved Block.

By the power of the Uncarved Block,
future generations would lessen their
selfish desires.
By lessening their selfish desires, the
world will move toward peace.

Part 2

Te Ching

Virtue Classic - Chapters 38 to 81

Chapter 38

The true good comes not from seeking
it, but from naturally becoming it.
An ordinary man seeks good, yet his
good is not constant.

The Master does not force virtue on
others,
so is able to bring about good in others.
The ordinary person who uses force
will accomplish nothing of lasting value.

The benevolent man acts from no hidden
motives.
The righteous person acts from
impersonal motives.
The dutiful person will act out of rules,
and when no one responds will roll up
his sleeves and use force.

When the Tao is forgotten, there is
righteousness.
When righteousness is forgotten, there
is duty.
When duty is forgotten, there is the
law.
The law is the shell of loyalty and faith,
and lack of loyalty and faith is the
beginning of chaos.

Our base beliefs come not from the Tao
but from the depths of
misunderstanding.
The Master lives in the fruit and not in
the husk.
The Tao is his abode, not the things that
hide it.
In so doing he rises to a greater wisdom.

Chapter 39

The ancient masters attained unity with the Tao.
Heaven gaining unity became pure.
Earth gained unity and discovered peace.
Spirits gained unity and received their potency.
Valleys gained unity and become full.
Humanity gained unity and was reborn.
Leaders in virtue of the Tao became examples to their empire.
The power of the Tao makes them what they are.

Without unity, Heaven becomes unclean.
Without unity, Earth becomes tremulous.
Without unity, spirits become vapors and disappear.
Without unity, valleys dry and crust.
Without unity, humanity fails to reproduce and perishes.
Without unity, leaders fail and become corrupted.

Therefore, the great have the small as
their root,
and the high must have the low as
foundation.
Leaders prize humility as their best
asset.
They call themselves alone and
disadvantaged.
Therefore attain honor with being
honored.
Do not shine like gemstones,
but be as dull as a grey stone.

Chapter 40

All actions end in the Tao.
Receptivity is the way of the Tao.

All creatures and all things spring from
the Tao.
Existence and non-existence are born of
the Tao.

Chapter 41

A superior person hears of the Tao and
enthusiastically practices it.
An average person hears of the Tao and
half believes.
A foolish person hears of the Tao and
sees it as a joke and laughs.
The laughter shows the humor of the
Tao.

Thus the old sayings:
The bright Tao appears dark.
The advancing Tao appears retreating.
The smooth path appears rough.
The superior way seems empty.

The pure seem soiled.
The true virtue appears to be lacking.
The virtue of care appears to be fear.

A great space has no corners,
the best vessels require the longest time
to complete,
the greatest sound cannot be heard,
and the greatest image has no form.

The Tao is hidden and nameless,
yet it alone always nourishes and
completes all creation.

Chapter 42

From the Tao came One.
From One came Two.
From Two came Three.
And from Three came all of creation.

The Yin is in all things.
The Yang is embraced by them.
The Yin and Yang together produce
harmony.

People don't want to be alone, suffering,
and disadvantaged.
But the true leaders take them as honor.
In loss, much can be gained.
In gain, much can be lost.

The lesson of others is also mine:
"Those who use power violently will die
unnaturally."

Chapter 43

Few in the world can comprehend
the teaching without words,
or understand the value of non-action.

Only a small few can comprehend
lessons without symbols, or grasp the
advantage of non-action.

Chapter 44

Which is dearer to you- your honor or your life?
Which is more valuable to you- your wealth or your person?
Which is more costly- gain or loss?

The greater the attachments, the greater the costs.
Amassing great fortune requires great loss.

Know your limits of possession to avoid dishonor,
and know when to stop to avoid pitfalls.

Chapter 45

The greatest achievements appear
incomplete,
yet their usefulness is constant.
The greatest fullness feels empty,
yet it will not be exhausted.

The greatest straightness seems
crooked.
The most valued skill seems like
clumsiness.
The greatest speech seems full of
stammers.

The straightest of straight appear
crooked.
The most skilled appear awkward.
The finest of speech seems stilted.

Agitation overcomes the cold,
and stillness overcomes the heat.
Purity and stillness is the world's ideal.

Chapter 46

The world in accord with the Tao:
horses run free yet fertilize the fields.
The world in discord with the Tao:
horses are bred for war outside the
cities.

Condoning the growth of people's selfish
desires leads to the greatest trespasses.
People's discontent lead to the greatest
disasters.
Greed will receive the greatest
retribution.

Those who are content are at peace
forever.

Chapter 47

Without opening your door,
you can know the whole world.
Without looking out your window,
you can understand the way of the Tao.

Behind closed doors is the whole world.
Without looking outside, you have the
Tao
to behold.

The increase of knowledge leads to
diminished comprehension.

The Master understands within her
dwelling, and
sees clearly without her eyes.
The Master accomplishes great things,
yet does nothing.

Chapter 48

One who seeks knowledge learns
something new every day.

The seeker of knowledge learns a lesson
each day.
The seeker of the Tao unlearns a lesson
each day.
Less and less remains until you arrive at
non-action.
When you arrive at non-action,
nothing will be left undone.

Lessons are unlearned until the arrival at
non-action.
Upon your arrival at non-action, nothing
will be left undone.

You master the world by letting the
world take its natural course.
There is no mastery by changing the
natural course of the world.

Chapter 49

The Master has no mind of his own.
He understands the mind of the people.

The Master thinks not of himself.
He understands the mind of the people.

The Master treats the good with good.
The Master treats the not good with
good.
In this way the Master gains true good.

To the trustworthy the Master gives
trust.
To the untrustworthy the Master gives
trust.
In this way the Master gains true trust.

The Master is shut off from the world.
The world is contained within his mind.
The people look to him for direction.
The interaction is fresh as with infants.

Chapter 50

Those who leave the womb at birth
and those who enter their source at
death,
of these; three out of ten celebrate life,
three out of ten celebrate death,
and three out of ten simply go from life
to death.
What is the reason for this?
Because they are afraid of dying,
Therefore they cannot live.

I have heard that those who celebrate
life
walk safely among the wild animals.
When they go into battle, they remain
unharmed.
The animals find no place to attack
them
and the weapons are unable to harm
them.
Why? Because they can find no place for
death in them.

Chapter 51

The Tao is the beginning of all creation.
The virtue of the Tao sustains them in nature
and their families gave them their forms.
Their environments then acted upon them to completion.
This is why all creatures respect the Tao and value its virtue.

All creatures respect the Tao and value its virtue, naturally without prompting.
Thus the Tao produces and its virtue cultivates, cares for, nurtures, nourishes, protects, and shelters.

It produces without possessing,
cares for without expectation,
nurtures without dominating,
This is called the dark and mysterious power.

Chapter 52

The world had a beginning
which we call the Great Mother.

Having discovered the Mother we can
know what her children should be.

When we know who the Mother is,
we begin to retain the qualities of the
Mother in us.
She will protect us from all danger even
after death.

Speak few words and take to a simple
life,
and you will have a life unburdened until
your last days.
If you should use words into a better
life,
there your troubles will mount without
end.

Understanding the small is called
resolution.
Knowing how to yield is called strength.

Using your inner light to understand without concern for pitfalls is called using the Absolute.

Chapter 53

If I understood only one thing,
I would use it to follow the Tao.
My one fear would be not letting go.

The Tao exists in level places,
but people will take short cuts.
Too much time spent fixing the house
means the land is neglected and full of
weeds,
and the granaries will soon become
empty
because there is no one out working the
fields.

Fancy clothes and adornments,
excessive eating and drinking,
hoarding loot and possessions,
This is a kind of theft and over-
consumption.

The Tao is in conflict with such
behaviors!

Chapter 54

The well-made product lasts into the generations.
That which is firmly anchored cannot slip away.
Those with excellent skills reach into posterity.

If this idea is cultivated in the individual,
then his virtue will become genuine.
Cultivation in the person makes genuine virtue.
Cultivation in the family makes great virtue.
Cultivation in the community multiplies virtue.
Cultivation in the country takes virtue far abroad.
Cultivation in the world makes virtue universal.

Then the character of the person is shown by the person.

The character of the family is shown by
the family.
The character of the community is
shown by the community.
The character of the country is shown by
the country.
The character of the world is shown by
the world.
How do I know this is so?
By observing these things.

Chapter 55

One who is filled with the Tao is like a young child.
Insects do not sting him, wild animals do not pounce upon him, and birds of prey do not attack him.
His bones are supple, his muscles soft, but his grip is tight and resolute.
He is not yet aware of the union of male and female,
but his member is stirred.
He cries all day and the voice stays strong.
He is in complete, natural harmony.
To understand harmony is to understand the eternal.
To know the eternal is to be discerning.
To artificially try to prolong life is not appropriate.
To alter natural flow of life's breath is unnatural.
The Master understands that creatures at their prime soon begin their decline.
To replace the natural with the unnatural is against the way of the Tao.

—

Those who combat the nature of the Tao
will perish early.

Chapter 56

Those who know are silent.
Those who are vocal do not know.

Quiet your talking,
close your ears,
soften your sharp movements,
let go your frustrations,
see with your inner light,
and submerge the turmoil.
This is called the mysterious unity.

Those who attain the mysterious unity
can neither be challenged nor
reproached.
They are not awarded nor harmed.
They are free from ennoblement and
dishonor.
This makes them noble under Heaven.

Chapter 57

Rule your country with virtue,
Arms are used with deception,
but the loyalty of allies and countrymen
are won by not-doing.
How do I know this is so?

Through this:
More prohibitions make people poorer.
More armaments put the country in
disorder.
More knowledge makes the world more
alien.
More laws and statutes increase crimes
and theft.

I do not meddle in their personal lives,
and the people become prosperous.
I let go of all my desires,
and the people return to the Uncarved
Block.

So the Master says:
I do not act, and the people become
good.

I am silent, and the people find their own answers.
I do not meddle and the people become prosperous.
I lose my desires and the people find their simplicity and honesty by themselves.

Chapter 58

In a listless governance,
the people are best provided.
In a powerful government,
the people become treacherous.

Good fortune finds its beginnings in
disaster,
and disaster stalks good fortune.
Good turns to bad, bad luck can turn
into
benefit.
Who can change the course, who can
anticipate
the change?
The delusion of control has long existed.

Thus the Master changes things with no
interference. He probes but does not
harm.

He is frank, yet his will is not a burden.
He shines, but is not harsh to behold.

Chapter 59

In moderation people learn the ways of
Heaven.
In moderation people are on the road to
the Tao.

Those who follow the Tao early
will have an abundance of virtue.

Begin early with the Tao and you end
with a surplus of virtue.
With a surplus of virtue, all things can be
accomplished.
With no limits on ability, Heaven is
within your reach.
When you understand the Mother of
Heaven, you will
long endure.

This is the way of the deep root and
strong trunk, the Way to a long life and
vision without limit.

Chapter 60

Govern a large country as you would a small fish.
Too much poking ruins it.

If the Tao is in governance, evil will lose its power.
Though evil will remain, its potency will be greatly diminished.

By avoiding violent ways, the Master disarms evil.
By not feeding evil, virtue will triumph.

Chapter 61

The large country is like a low lying river.
The world comes to it like waters.
The large country should be serene and humble,
as the female overcomes the male with serenity.

If the large country is lower than it can relate to the smaller country.
If the smaller country is lower than it may be overwhelmed.
In adopting the lower position the large country protects the small while receiving the benefits of the small country.

Large countries seek to gain and protect people.
Small countries seek to join and serve people.
So both gain from by the lower position of the large country.

Chapter 62

The Tao is the highest spirit of creation;
It is the treasure for the good man.
It is the refuge for the bad man.

Gain can be had by speech.
Improvements can be made by deeds.
But even the bad cannot entirely forsake
the Tao.

When a new leader takes office,
don't give him gifts and offerings.
These things are not as valuable
as teaching him about the Tao.

A new leader is given gifts and offerings.
None of them can be as valuable as the
lessons

of the Tao.

Why was the Tao esteemed by the
ancient Masters?
Is it not said: "With it we find without
searching.
With it we find forgiveness for our
transgressions."
That is why the world cannot under
stand it.

Why did the ancient Masters esteem the
Tao so?
Because with the Tao they sought and
found.
With the Tao they were forgiven for their
failings.
The Tao is precious for all.

Chapter 63

Act without action.
Manage without meddlesomeness.
Take pleasure in the ordinary and
simple.
See the vastness in the small.
Solve difficulties when they are still
easy.
Large problems are solved in pieces.
Great undertakings begin in small steps.
The Master never undertakes too much
at once,
so he achieves beyond expectation.

When an affirmation is given too lightly,
keep your eyes open for trouble ahead.
When praise is given breezily,
get your attention focused more.
When an endeavor looks easy,
problems are hidden away.

The Master expecting great difficulties,
readies herself for unexpected
difficulties.

Chapter 64

Things are easier to control while things
are quiet.
Things are easier to plan far in advance.

Quiet and stillness are the times to
manage.
Long range plans address small
occurrences.
Break things when they are still brittle.
Small things are easily vanished.

Solve problems in their early stages.
The mighty tree was once a miniscule
tip.
A journey of a thousand miles initiates
with one
single step.

If you hurry into action, failure follows.
If you hold too tightly, your grip
becomes weak.
So the Master allows the course of
things and doesn't fail.

She doesn't seize things so never loses them.
She follows through to the end as much as the beginning and errors are prevented.
The Master thinks not of possessing.
She learns by learning and unlearning.
Thus she is able to comprehend all things.
This gives her the power to help all creation.

Chapter 65

The ancient Masters didn't instruct people, but let them be simple in themselves.

An excess of cleverness in people is a barrier to good governing.
Therefore, avoid cleverness in ruling a country.
Rulers who forgo cleverness in rule are blessings to the state.

Keep this understanding as a guide and rule.
The knowledge of this guide and rule is a virtue.
It is a mysterious virtue.
It is goes against our mind's tendencies, but harmonizes the state with the Tao.

Chapter 66

Receiving the flow of hundreds of
streams, the rivers and seas are the
rulers.
They receive the flow because of their
low position.

Wishing to be the leader, you must
speak as though you are the follower.
Wishing to lead others, you must follow
them.

A wise leader with her power does not
create feelings of burden among her
people.

In her position as leader, the people will
not feel her weight or feel manipulated.

The whole world will seek her help and
not tire of her.
Because she does not compete no one
can compete with what she
accomplishes.

Chapter 67

The whole world speaks reverently to me
of the Tao,
yet their actions belie their words.
The world belittles what is seen as great.
The Tao is too easy they say.

I have only three treasures that I keep
and cherish.
They are compassion, conservation, and
humility.
Compassion enables bravery.
Conservation enables giving.
Humility enables great leadership.

A compassionless bravery, liberality
without conserving, or leadership
without humility will only lead to much
strife.
The soldier with compassion will gain
victory.
And compassion will secure your
defenses.
Heaven itself protects those with
compassion.

Chapter 68

The best soldiers shun violence.
The best generals are disinclined to
destruction.
The best strategists avoid confrontation.
The best leaders are like servants of
their people.

This is called the virtue of non-
contentiousness.
This is called the power of using other's
efforts.
This is called the sublimity of Heaven.

Chapter 69

The military has a saying:
"I dare not take the role of the host, but rather that of the guest. Better to retreat a foot than to advance only an inch."

This is called gathering power in retreat, pushing without force, and defeating the enemy without battle.

It is a great disaster to underestimate your enemy. Underestimating your enemy is like losing your great advantage.
When equal forces meet in battle,
the side with greater compassion wins.

Chapter 70

My words are very easy to understand and to practice.
Yet no one in the world seems able to understand them.
No one seems to practice what I teach.

My teachings come form old sources, and they are grounded in principles.

There are only a few who know me, so only a few who understand my teachings.
Because those who know me are few, my teachings become even more precious.

Chapter 71

Knowing you don't know is wholeness.
Thinking you know is an impairment.
Recognize that you have this flaw and seek
to be rid of it.

The Master is whole.
He knows his impairments and rids them,
and is able to remain whole.

Chapter 72

When people are too bold, they invite
disaster.
Do not meddle with people's means.
Respect their means and the people will
respect you.

Therefore, the Master knows himself but
makes no show.
He loves both himself and others.
This is how discards the valueless and
keeps the valuable.

Chapter 73

Those that dare boldly will not survive.
Those that dare in caution will last.

One is the way of death.
The other is the path to living.
The workings of Heaven are subtle.

The Tao of the universe
does not compete, yet wins;
does not speak, yet has the answers;
does not command, yet leads;
and does not act, but completes.

Heaven's nets are vast,
yet nothing can slip through.

Chapter 74

If you are not afraid of dying,
you are not under death's control.
If there is no fear of death,
you are free and capable of anything.

Without that fear you are able to shear
away
the useless parts of your own life like
a great carpenter who has learned to cut
with experience and is not afraid of
mistakes.

Chapter 75

When the government taxes too much
people go hungry,
When the government meddles too
much,
the people become restless.

When the wealthy have too much,
people begin to view death lightly,
this cause more poverty.

Those who do not clasp onto life can
save their lives.

Chapter 76

Living bodies are soft and flexible;
Dead bodies are rigid and hard.
Living plants are pliable and moist;
Dead ones are brittle and dried.

Those who are rigid and hard
are following the dead.
Those who are soft and flexible
are following the living.

The rigid and hard will break.
The brittle and dried will crumble.
Follow the living by being soft and
pliable.
This is the way of victory.

Chapter 77

When a bow is drawn, the top is bent down,
and the bottom is bent up.
This is like the action of the Tao of Heaven
on Earth.
Things are balanced from excess to the deficient.

The way of the Tao works to use the excess,
and gives to that which is depleted.
The way of people is to take from the depleted,
and give more to those with excess.

Who can give up his excess and give it to the lacking?
Only those who are with the Tao.

This is why the Master gives freely.
She takes no credit, gives humbly, and is not

in need of praise.

Chapter 78

The softest and most flexible substance
is water.
Yet nothing can resist or overcome
water.

Everyone knows that the soft and
yielding
overcomes the rigid and hard,
yet only a few will apply this knowledge.

The Master says the humble servant of
the country is worthy to rule.
The one willing to take on the low,
inglorious tasks makes the best ruler.

True sayings seem like paradoxes.

Chapter 79

Resolving a dispute may still leave
resentments.
What good can come from this?

Therefore the Master upholds his side
and makes no demands of others.
The virtuous person does the right thing.
Persons without virtue look only for
selfish advantage.

The Tao does not choose sides;
the good person receives from the Tao
because he is on its side.

The Tao does not favor sides;
the virtuous person receives from the
Tao
from virtue.

Chapter 80

Small countries with small populations
are good.
Give them new technologies and luxuries
and they see that these things are not
necessary.
Teach them that death is grave and to
be content
in their homes.

Though they may have many horses,
wagons, and boats, they are satisfied
by staying put.
Though they have arms and defenses,
they will not display them.

Allow people to enjoy the work of their
hands,
the consumption of hearty food,
the making of their own clothes,
the contentment of being in their homes,
the delight of their country's customs.

Though the neighbor country may be so close that their roosters and dogs can be heard,
the people are content never to visit each other.

Chapter 81

True words aren't dressed in beauty.
Beautiful words lose the true.

The wise don't have points to assert.
And those who assert are not wise.

Wise men do not over value scholarship,
and scholarship does not make wise.

The Master doesn't desire possessions.

The Master desires no possessions.
She gains in the service of others and
has more than she needs.
And the more she gives, the more she
receives.

The Tao of Heaven gives freely without
force.
The wise in possessing the Tao act
without contention.

11032556R00066